# Nelson

## SPELLING

# PUPIL BOOK 4

## JOHN JACKMAN

### Nelson

# Book 4 – Contents/Scope and Sequence

| Page | Focus | Extra | Extension | Focus pcm | Extension pcm |
|------|-------|-------|-----------|-----------|---------------|
| 4/5 Unit 1 | Flashback! Review all Book 3 patterns | y adjectives y + ier/iest ending patterns en/on endings | plurals y adjectives y + ier/iest silent letters roots/prefixes/ suffixes | | |
| 6/7 Unit 2 | ness, ment | y ending + ness y ending + ment | cess words | adding ness/ment cloze sentence writing | syllables |
| 8/9 Unit 3 | sure, ture cloze | root words | related words with ure | ture pattern word building word/picture matching | hidden words definitions/puzzle |
| 10/11 Unit 4 | sion | ersion, ision, ension patterns | ssion words | ision, usion, ension pattern cloze hidden words puzzle | making sion nouns from verbs |
| 12/13 Unit 5 | tion | unction, ection, action, uction patterns | tion abstract nouns | action, ection, uction pattern cloze hidden words puzzle | making tion nouns from verbs |
| 14/15 Unit 6 | ph wordsearch | ph or f? | Greek ph words | ph pattern word building word/picture matching | ph or gh? silent p and silent h sentence writing |
| 16/17 Unit 7 | al endings | al adjectives | ally adverbs | tal, dal endings word building | l or ll? adding ly sentence writing |
| 18/19 Unit 8 | el endings cloze | nnel | il, vel, rel, attle, dle, tal, ual, ile endings | single word comprehension word/picture matching | selecting el, le, al dictionary definitions |
| 20/21 | *Check-up 1* | *Check-up 1* | *Check-up 1* | *Check-up 1* | *Check-up 1* |
| 22/23 Unit 9 | ough | similar-sounding words | ough, augh | adding ough/ought cloze sentence writing | jumbled ough words homophones |
| 24/25 Unit 10 | ea rhyme | hidden ea words | ea with the sound of a in 'make' | ead/eather patterns word/picture matching | word/clue matching sentence writing |

| Page | Focus | Extra | Extension | Focus pcm | Extension pcm |
|---|---|---|---|---|---|
| 26/27 Unit 11 | soft c | ance, ence, ince | adding ing | rhyme puzzle sorting by ence, ince, ance | adding ence, ance dictionary definitions word families |
| 28/29 Unit 12 | dge | adding ing/d | dge/ge patterns | rhyme puzzle sorting by udge, edge, idge sentence writing | dge/age word/definition matching sentence writing |
| 30/31 Unit 13 | er, or, ar endings | cloze | alphabetical ordering of same-family words | word/clue matching word/picture matching | selecting er, or, ar dictionary checking and definitions |
| 32/33 Unit 14 | ary, ery, ory endings wordsearch | roots/word building | making plurals | word/picture matching sorting by ary, ery, ory | word building puzzle root words |
| 34/35 Unit 15 | un, en, in, im prefixes | prefix puzzle | prefixes and doubled letters | single word comprehension word/picture matching | identifying prefixes Greek prefixes (tele–, mono–, auto–, dia–) |
| 36/37 | *Check-up 2* | *Check-up 2* | *Check-up 2* | *Check-up 2* | *Check-up 2* |
| 38/39 Unit 16 | ous, ious cloze | matching nouns and adjectives | our/orous rule ous/ious pattern | adding ous/ious cloze sentence writing | root nouns sorting adjectives by ous, ious, eous, orous sorting adverbs by ously, iously, eously, orously |
| 40/41 Unit 17 | a and double letters | doubled consonant puzzle box | syllables | ann, app, arr, att, ass, acc patterns word/picture matching | selecting correct double consonant spellings |
| 42/43 Unit 18 | ent, ence ant, ance cloze | matching nouns and adjectives | making and using adverbs | simple ent/ant crossword sentence writing | selecting ent, ence, ant, ance dictionary checking and definitions |
| 44/45 Unit 19 | tricky words 1 | ie/ei rule | double consonant problems | adiing silent w, u sorting by silent w, h, b, k | editing for spelling |
| 46/47 Unit 20 | tricky words 2 contractions | e + able | Greek problems! | writing/matching contractions | Greek and Latin root words |
| 48 | *Check-up 3* | *Check-up 3* | *Check-up 3* | *Check-up 3* | *Check-up 3* |

# Flashback!

## *Focus* FLASHBACK

Find the missing letters.
Copy the words into your book.

1 m____

2 gl____

3 b____

4 s____

5 w____

6 p____

7 t____

8 r____

9 q____

10 s____

11 y____

12 sh____

13 k____

14 b____

15 gh____

16 f____

17 g____

18 g____

19 c____

20 sh____

21 e____

22 t____

23 d____

24 m____

25 h____

You may need to double the last letter of some of the words.

**A** Make adjectives ending in **y** from these words.

1 wind    2 rock    3 fun    4 sleep

5 sun    6 spot    7 creak    8 storm

**B** Change these words into two comparing words that end with **ier** or **iest**.

1 windy    2 cloudy    3 rainy    4 chilly

**C** Copy these words into your book. Look at their endings. Underline the odd one out in each set.

1 *magnet cabinet tablet bonnet*

2 *wicket helmet cricket bucket*

**D** Finish these words with *en* or *on*.

1 one more than six *sev__*    2 fastens clothes *butt__*    3 a young cat *kitt__*

You may need to drop the last letter of some of the words!

**A** Write the plural form of these nouns.

1 flask   2 class   3 bus   4 glass   5 baby   6 ditch

**B** Make adjectives ending in **y** from these words.

1 dirt    2 wave    3 smoke    4 dust

5 laze    6 noise    7 stone    8 bone

**C** Change these words into two comparing words that end with **ier** or **iest**.

1 pretty    2 sleep    3 silly    4 messy

**D** Copy these words, adding the missing silent letter in each.

1 *r_yme*    2 *_onest*    3 *clim_*    4 *_nee*    5 *si_n*    6 *colum_*

**E** Copy these words into your book. Underline the root word and circle any prefixes and suffixes.

1 *reminded*    2 *unwinding*    3 *rewinding*    4 *unkindly*

# ness
# ment

**key words**

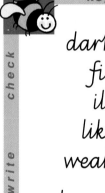

darkness
fitness
illness
likeness
weakness

happiness
laziness
silliness
ugliness

agreement
department
enjoyment
statement

*look say cover write check* (×2, running down both sides)

**A** Which key word does each picture remind you of?

**B** Look at these words.

> ill enjoy blind agree quiet treat
> bright pay fit state dark punish

You can add **ness** to some, and you can add **ment** to others. Make two lists, one for each type.

6

Listen carefully to the sound of the **y** before deciding whether to change it!

Remember: to add a suffix to a word that ends in **y**, where the **y** sounds like **ee** in 'bee', change the **y** to an **i** and add the suffix, like this:

ug**ly**   ugl**i**ness;    merry   merr**i**ment

Add *ness* or *ment* to each of these words and then use four of the new words in sentences.

1 lazy     2 naughty     3 nasty     4 empty     5 enjoy

6 pay     7 happy     8 heavy     9 dry     10 pretty

Here are some different **ess** words.

When trying to remember a difficult word it sometimes helps to look for a smaller word inside the bigger one.
**Necessary** is a difficult word to spell until you remember it has a **cess** pit in the middle of it!
(A **cess pit** is where sewage is pumped if there is no main drainage!)

Here are some more **cess** words.

| excessive recess procession abscess unnecessary concession successful |
| --- |

Copy the words, then put each of them into a sentence to show what it means. Use a dictionary to help you.

7

# sure

# ture

For bumble bees just live for plea**sure**
And never work a single day,
Oh what a lovely life of lei**sure**
Just to buzz around and play.

Jeremy Lloyd

## SPELLING *Focus*

### key words

**check**  **look**

measure
treasure
leisure

**write**  **say**

displeasure
exposure

**cover**  **cover**

future
mixture
nature
picture

**say**  **write**

puncture
texture
fracture

**look**  **check**

adventure

Copy these sentences. Use a word from the box to fill each gap.

| creature picture capture nature |
|---|

"Look at that little _____," said Bob.

"It's a spider," said his teacher. "Will you draw a _____ of it?"

"Look, it's spinning a web to help it _____ a fly," said Bob.

"Isn't it marvellous how _____ works?" said Mr Chaudhri.

"Yes, as long as you're not a fly!" thought Bob.

**A** Match each of the words in the list with the shorter word from which it has been made.
Copy the two lists of words into your book.
Draw neat lines to join the related words.
One is done to help you.

enclose          failure

fail          pleasure

depart          enclosure

moist          pressure

furnish          departure

press          furniture

please          moisture

**B** Write sentences to use three of these **ure** words.

Look at the words in the box.

> futuristic featuring endurance
> security lecturer torturing
> pressurised insurance agricultural
> natural picturesque moist

Each one has a related word with a **ure** ending.
Write out the words in the box, and next to each, the related **ure** word. The first is done to help you.

1 futuristic future

# sion

diver**sion**

## SPELLING *Focus*

**key words**

look say cover write check

*look say cover write check*

vision
television
revision
division

invasion
occasion

version
diversion
excursion

pension
extension
comprehension

**A** Match a key word to each of these pictures.
Write the answers in your book.

1 _____   2 _____   3 _____

4 _____   5 _____   6 _____

**B** Write sentences about three of the pictures.

**A** Find two words that rhyme with each of these words. Write them in your book.

version      television      pension

**B** Write a short passage of not more than three sentences. Each sentence must include at least one of the key words.

SPELLING *Extension*

**A** Read the words in the box and the list of definitions. Then match each word to its definition. Copy them into your book. The first is done for you.

---

*passion  compassion  discussion  concussion  percussion*

*concession  permission  admission  possession  profession*

---

1 talking over something
2 pity, sympathy or mercy
3 a strong feeling, such as love or hate
4 something granted as part of a bargain
5 dazed feeling caused by a blow
6 freedom to do something
7 a noisy striking
8 having as one's own
9 an occupation requiring a lot of training
10 letting people enter

1 *discussion*

11

# tion

station

## SPELLING *Focus*

### key words

*look say cover write check*

station
relation
question
education

action
fraction
attraction

election
section
direction

suction
destruction
instruction

*look say cover write check*

Match a key word to each of the pictures.

1 _____

2 _____

3 _____

4 _____

5 _____

6 _____

7 _____

8 _____

9 _____

> *function section connection attraction direction*
> *suction junction election infection objection selection*
> *destruction subtraction instruction*

**A**  The words in the box all end with **ction**, but there are four rhyming groups. Write them in the four lists below. One group is much bigger than the other three.

| *function* | *section* | *attraction* | *suction* |
|---|---|---|---|

**B**  Choose one word from each list and put it in a sentence.

SPELLING *Extension*

Notice that the final **e** is dropped before **tion** is added.

**Abstract nouns** name things we cannot see, touch, hear, taste or smell.

Abstract nouns are often made by adding **tion** or **sion** to a verb. If the verb ends with **ate**, the abstract noun will end with **tion**.

  Examples: educ**ate**  educa**tion**

The 'shun' sound at the end of a word is nearly always spelt **tion**. Never spell it with **sh** except in 'fashion' and 'cushion'.

**A**  Use a dictionary to help you make the abstract noun to go with each of these verbs.

1 relate      2 operate      3 create      4 calculate

5 situate     6 evaporate    7 inspire     8 express

9 discuss    10 prepare     11 circulate  12 observe

The last three are tricky! A dictionary might help.

**B**  Write the verbs related to these abstract nouns.

1 composition  2 opposition  3 direction  4 action

5 pollution      6 solution    7 reception  8 detention

13

# ph

dolphin

elephant

pheasant

photo

phantom

SPELLING *Focus*

**key words**

*look   say   cover   write   check*

*check   write   cover   say   look*

graph
phantom
pheasant
phone
photo
physical

alphabet
dolphin
elephant
geography
microphone
pamphlet
prophet
sphere

**A** There are ten **ph** key words hidden in this puzzle. Write them in your book.

| a | p | h | a | n | t | o | m | b | g | p |
|---|---|---|---|---|---|---|---|---|---|---|
| k | l | m | l | c | h | g | r | a | p | h |
| e | l | e | p | h | a | n | t | e | h | e |
| m | r | p | h | o | n | e | d | f | o | a |
| t | s | p | a | m | p | h | l | e | t | s |
| w | x | i | b | o | p | q | n | u | o | a |
| a | z | v | e | d | o | l | p | h | i | n |
| j | b | y | t | p | r | o | p | h | e | t |

**B** Write a sentence that uses two **ph** words.

14

In most words **ph** sounds like **f**. In this list of words all the **ph**'s are written with an **f**, but be careful – a few of the **f**'s should be there!
Write the words correctly in your book.`

1 alfabet    2 telefone    3 before    4 dolfin

5 sfere    6 geografy    7 pamflet    8 difficult

9 profet    10 fotograf    11 triumf    12 fysical

Most words that start with, or contain, **ph** are words now used in English that came from the Greek language.

Examples: **phone** – Greek for *voice* or *sound*
           **graph** – Greek for *writing*
           **sphere** – Greek for *ball*
           **photo** – Greek for *light*

**A** Sort the words in the box into the lists according to their Greek root word.

One word can go into two lists.

> autograph sphere microphone
> atmosphere photograph telephone
> graph hemisphere paragraph
> saxophone telegraph

| graph | sphere | phone | photo |

**B** Without using a dictionary, choose four of the words and write a definition of each, using what you have been told about their Greek origins.

**C** Find at least two more to add to each list.

# al
## endings

medal

## SPELLING *Focus*

### key words

| |
|---|
| look say cover write check |

medal
metal
pedal
petal
sandal
signal
medical
hospital
accidental
special
usual
occasional

**A** Match a key word to each of these pictures.
Write the answers in your book.

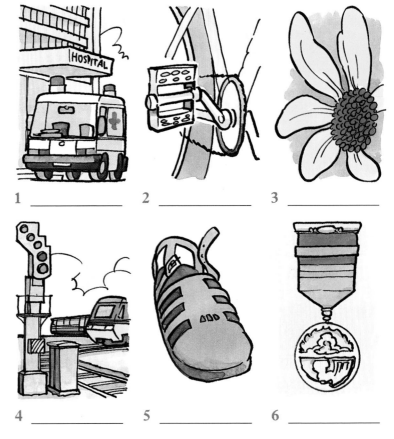

1 _____  2 _____  3 _____

4 _____  5 _____  6 _____

**B** Write sentences about three of the pictures.

Many words that end in **al** are adjectives.

Example: dentist (noun)   dental (adjective)

Check your answers
in a dictionary.

**A** For each of these nouns, write the related adjective.

1 nature    2 fact     3 medicine   4 centre

5 music    6 history   7 accident   8 bride

9 comic    10 mechanic

**B** For each of these adjectives, write the related noun.

1 occasional     2 national     3 topical

4 additional     5 original

SPELLING *Extension*

Many adverbs end in **ly**. When adding an **ly** ending to a word ending in **al**, don't be tempted to drop one of the **l**'s. You need them both!

**A** Copy and finish this chart.

| noun | adjective | adverb |
|---|---|---|
| norm | normal | normally |
| nation | | |
| origin | | |
| accident | | |
| act | actual | |
| event | | |
| use | | |

**B** What do you notice about the last three?

17

# el
## endings

SPELLING *Focus*

### key words

camel
panel
chapel
gravel
travel
chisel
jewel
novel

cancel
satchel
kestrel
tinsel
mongrel
hostel
cockerel

*look say cover write check* (vertical, both sides)

**A** Find eight key words that are shown in the picture.

**B** Which key words are missing from the gaps?
Write them in your book.

A ____1____ is hovering overhead. It is watching the
mouse as it scavenges food from the man's ____2____.
The bird is about to dive when the ____3____ crows
and frightens the mouse, who startles the man, who
drops his ____4____ , just missing the ____5____ dog,
who decides he'll find somewhere more peaceful
to sleep!

All the answers to these clues end with the letters **nnel**.

1 You might use this when you wash in the morning.

2 This is a narrow stretch of sea, as between England and France.

3 Many ships have one or more.

4 It carries roads or railways through mountains.

5 It's a dog's house you can keep in the garden.

Look carefully at the endings of the words in the box.
They all have an **l**.
Sort them into eight sets to make three of a kind.
The first is done to help you.

| | | | | |
|---|---|---|---|---|
| candle | fossil | hostile | casual | gravel |
| cattle | total | nostril | kestrel | tonsil |
| agile | cradle | battle | factual | postal |
| | mongrel | novel | cockerel | rattle |
| travel | needle | mental | actual | fertile |

1 *fossil nostril tonsil*

19

# Check-up 1

**A** Write the word that goes with each picture.
The first few letters are given to help you.

1  *mea*_____

2  *trea*_____

3  *pic*_____

4  *punc*_____

5  *tele*_____

6  *sta*_____

7  *ques*_____

8  *frac*_____

9  *dol*_____

10  *ele*_____

11  *med*_____

12  *pet*_____

13  *sig*_____

14  *cam*_____

15  *jew*_____

16  *chis*_____

**B** Write a short story, using at least six of the words from A.

**C** **Elephant** has **ph** that sounds like **f**.
Write four more words that have **ph** that sounds like **f**.

20

**A** Add *ness* or *ment* to each of these words.

1 punish   2 pay   3 enjoy   4 happy   5 lazy

6 merry   7 ugly   8 heavy   9 pretty   10 empty

**B** Copy these words, and next to each, write the root word from which it comes. The first is done to help you.

1 *pressure* *press*   2 *enclosure*

3 *failure*   4 *departure*   5 *pleasure*

**C** Finish each of these words, using *tion* or *sion*.

1 *divi____*   2 *educa____*   3 *inva____*   4 *suc____*

5 *pen____*   6 *elec____*   7 *diver____*   8 *instruc____*

**D** Add *f* or *ph* to complete these words.

1 *___lower*   2 *___one*   3 *___otogra___*   4 *help___ul*

5 *al___abet*   6 *___ysical*   7 *___isherman*   8 *pam___let*

**A** Write two more words in each of these word families. The first is done to help you.

1 necessary *unnecessary   necessarily*

2 success   3 excess   4 process

**B** Write the abstract noun (that ends with **ion**) which is related to each of these.

1 operate   2 discuss   3 express   4 provide

5 create   6 admit   7 pollute   8 compose

9 decide   10 submit

**C** What does each of these words mean in the Greek language?

1 sphere   2 phone   3 photo   4 graph

# ough

The sea can be angry
The sea can be **rough**
The sea can be vicious
The sea can be **tough**.

John Foster

## SPELLING *Focus*

### key words

look say cover write check

rough
enough

cough
trough

dough
though

nought
bought
brought
thought

bough
plough

look say cover write check

Which key word does each picture remind you of?
Write them in your book.

1

2

3

4  2 - 2 = ?

5

6

7

8

9

These sets of words have very similar sounds, and so can cause spelling problems.

**A** Copy these sentences neatly into your book, selecting the correct words.

*It was a rough/ruff morning. Bows/Boughs were falling from the trees, but the baker fort/fault/fought his way to the village bakery. He knew his hot, crusty bread was much sought/sort after by the tourists, and no sooner had he started baking his first batch of doe/dough than he saw his first customers of the day peeping in threw/through his window.*

**B** Use a dictionary to check your answers.

## SPELLING *Extension*

**A 1** Write two words where the **ough** sounds like the **uff** in **fluff**.

**2** Write two words where the **ough** sounds like **off**.

**3** Write two words where the **ough** sounds like the **ow** in **snow**.

**4** Write two words where the **ough** sounds like the **ow** in **how**.

**B** Beware! The letter pattern **augh** can sometimes make a similar sound to **ough** (as in **bought**), or sometimes it sounds like **ar** in **park**.

*laughter taught caught laugh daughter slaughter laughing naughty draughts*

Sort these nine words into two sets according to the sound made by the **augh** letter pattern.

Write an amusing nonsense sentence using as many of the **augh** words as you can manage.

bread

# ea

SPELLING *Focus*

### key words

*look say cover write check*

dead
head
read
bread
tread
health
wealth
spread
feather
leather
weather
ready
steady
wealthy

*look say cover write check*

**A** Look at the pictures.
Write the rhyming key words they give clues to.
The first one is done to help you.

1 **weather** rhymes with  *feather*

2 **tread** rhymes with

3 **thread** rhymes with

4 **steady** rhymes with

5 **healthy** rhymes with

**B** Write five other **ea** key words that sound like **e** in **bed**.

**C** Write the key words that can be said in more than one way.

Find and copy into your book the 11 **ea** words hidden in the puzzle.

| b | g | p | m | h | e | a | d | j |
|---|---|---|---|---|---|---|---|---|
| d | p | l | e | a | s | u | r | e |
| t | r | e | a | s | u | r | e | a |
| h | b | a | s | i | c | k | a | l |
| r | r | s | u | a | l | e | d | o |
| e | e | a | r | n | f | j | y | u |
| a | a | n | e | d | e | a | d | s |
| d | d | t | r | e | a | d | h | m |

Sometimes **ea** can make the sound found in 'make'.
For example: break   great   steak

A   Complete these word webs, adding as many prefixes and suffixes or both, to see how many family words you can find.

*breakfast*

*break*          *great*   *greatness*

Remember, a **homophone** has a similar sound but different spelling and meaning.

B   Copy the three **ea** words from the box. Next to each one write a homophone. Write a nonsense sentence for each pair of homophones.

# soft C

procession

cymbal

police

certificate

camel

## key words

look say cover write check

centre
cement
certain
celebrate
certificate
ceremony

police
service

accident

advance
entrance
sentence
convince

look say cover write check

**A** Read these two words:

cymbals

clown

Listen to the sound the **c** makes.
The letter **c** in 'cymbals' is **soft** (like **s**).
The letter **c** in 'clown' is **hard**.

1 Look at the picture at the top of these pages.
Copy six **soft c** words.

2 Copy four **hard c** words from the picture.

3 Write the words in the picture which have both a **soft c** and a **hard c**.

**B** Write in your book the key words that match these clues.

1 law officers

2 persuade

3 sure

4 way in

5 middle

6 ends with a full stop

clown
circus
cedar
cricket
cattle
dance
casualty
control
canal
cycle

Add *ance, ence* or *ince* to make complete words.
Check your answers in a dictionary.

1 ch_____ 2 f_____ 3 s_____

4 m_____ 5 p_____ 6 pr_____

7 adv_____ 8 comm_____ 9 dist_____

10 entr_____ 11 sent_____ 12 off_____

If we add **ing** to words ending with **nce** we must first
drop the last **e**.

The men like to **dance**.
They like **dancing** together.

Add *ing* to each of these words.

1 fence       2 wince       3 pounce

4 bounce      5 prance      6 glance

7 commence  8 convince  9 announce

27

# dge

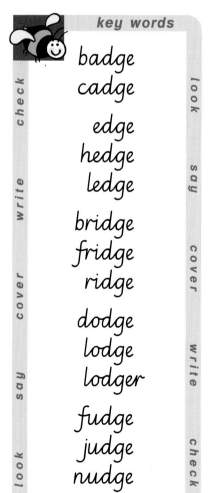

**key words**

look say cover write check

badge
cadge

edge
hedge
ledge

bridge
fridge
ridge

dodge
lodge
lodger

fudge
judge
nudge

look say cover write check

**A** Sort the words in the picture into these families.
Write them in your book.

| adge | edge | idge | odge | udge |

**B** How many words can you make by changing the first letter of **hedge**?

For example: *hedge   sledge*

Now try the same thing with **judge**.

28

**A** Copy and finish this chart.

|  | + ing | + d |
|---|---|---|
| cadge | cadging | cadged |
| hedge |  |  |
| bridge |  |  |
| dodge |  |  |
| judge |  |  |

**B** Write a sentence about the picture on page 28 using one of the **ing** words, and another using a **d** word.

SPELLING *Extension*

Not all the words that have a 'j' sound have the **dge** letter pattern. A **d** usually only goes before **ge** if it follows a short vowel sound, like this:

> badge, fu**d**ge (short vowel, **d**)
> page, huge (long vowel, so **no** d)

Beware! There are words with short vowels but no **d**, like these:

> village   garage   college   allege

**A** Copy ten of the key words. Underline the short vowel in each one.

**B** Write these words in your book. Some need a **d**, others don't. Use a dictionary to help you.

1 bri_____ crosses a river

3 oran_____ a fruit

5 nu_____ gentle shove

7 ra_____ violent anger

2 he_____ a row of bushes

4 fri_____ keeps food cool

6 stran_____ unusual

8 ba_____ a sign worn on clothes

# er or ar endings

**key words**

computer
newspaper
customer
stranger
builder

burglar
calendar
popular
particular
similar

interior
superior
calculator
radiator

*look · say · cover · write · check · look · say · cover · write · check*

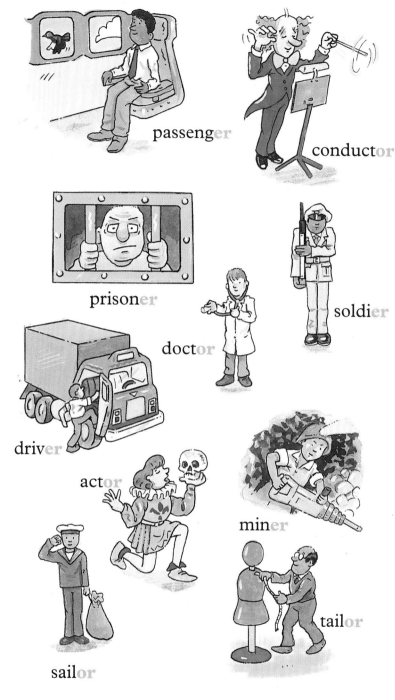

passenger

conductor

prisoner

soldier

doctor

driver

actor

miner

sailor

tailor

**A** Look at the last two letters in the words on the picture. Sort them into two groups.

**B** Write one sentence that has both an **er** ending word and an **or** ending word in it.

Copy these sentences into your book. Choose a key word to fill each gap.

My parents said they would buy me a ____ to help with my school work. As they are so expensive we looked for second-hand ones in the ____.

"Is there a ____ type you want?" asked Dad.

"No, but IBM computers are very ____," I said.

"Yes, it certainly seems a ____ make. There are lots in the paper," said Mum.

"This one looks good," I said. "It has a built-in ____ to give the date, and a ____ to work out all my maths homework for me!"

A Arrange these groups of words in alphabetical order. Write them in your book.

1 instructor instruct instruction instructed instructing
2 circular circle circled circulation circling
3 computer compute computation computerise computed
4 popular popularise population populated populate
5 calculator calculation calculate calculating calculated
6 customer customise customising customers custom

B Without using a dictionary, write a short definition of the first word in each group.

C Now look the word up in a dictionary.
Compare your definition with that in the dictionary. What other information does the dictionary give about each word?

# ory
# ary
# ery

story

jewell**ery**

diction**ary**

SPELLING *Focus*

**key words**

*look   say   cover   write   check*

story
factory
memory
history
victory

necessary
ordinary
dictionary
secretary
library
burglary

mystery
discovery
jewellery

*look   say   cover   write   check*

**A** Find in the wordsearch at least three words with each of these endings:

**ary   ery   ory**

Write them in your book.

| b | u | r | g | l | a | r | y | s |
|---|---|---|---|---|---|---|---|---|
| m | y | s | t | e | r | y | x | e |
| v | n | u | r | s | e | r | y | c |
| i | m | e | m | o | r | y | z | r |
| c | r | o | c | k | e | r | y | e |
| t | l | i | b | r | a | r | y | t |
| o | h | i | s | t | o | r | y | a |
| r | f | a | c | t | o | r | y | r |
| y | l | m | e | s | t | o | r | y |

**B** Write and illustrate in your book a funny nonsense sentence that uses at least three of the words from the box.

**A** Finish these words by adding *ory*, *ary* or *ery* to each one. Then use your dictionary and write a meaning for each word you have made.

1 hist_____          2 necess_____

3 diction_____          4 nurs_____

5 ordin_____          6 machin_____

7 fact_____          8 deliv_____

9 discov_____          10 mem_____

**B** Copy these words. Next to each one, write its root word. The first one is done to help you.

1 jewellery   jewel          2 machinery          3 bribery

4 observatory          5 discovery          6 nursery

7 slippery          8 brewery          9 delivery

To make plurals of words ending with **ory**, **ary** or **ery**, remember to change the **y** to **i** before adding **es**, like this: factory factor**ies**;   library librar**ies**

**A** Write the plural form of each of these words in your book.

1 secretary     2 memory     3 victory     4 dictionary

5 nursery     6 discovery     7 burglary     8 delivery

**B** Write in your book sentences which use the plural forms of these words, one sentence for each question. (You can write funny or silly sentences, but you mustn't miss out any of the words!)

1   secretary   burglary   dictionary

2   delivery   brewery   nursery

3   memory   story   victory

# un en in im

**in**correct

## SPELLING *Focus*

**key words**

look say cover write check

*undone*
*unhappy*
*unkind*
*untidy*

*enable*
*enclose*
*enlarge*

*inaccurate*
*incomplete*
*incorrect*
*invisible*

*imperfect*
*impossible*
*impure*

look say cover write check

**A** Match a key word to each of these pictures.
Write the answers in your book.

1 *un*_____   2 *un*_____   3 *en*_____

4 *in*_____   5 *in*_____   6 *im*_____

**B** Write sentences using two of these words.

**A** Write the key word answers to these puzzles in your book.

1 can't be seen         in _____

2 to make possible    en _____

3 things not neatly put away   un _____

4 miserable            un _____

5 wrong              in _____

6 not quite right      in _____

7 to make bigger      en _____

**B** Use a dictionary to find the meanings of these words:
1 endeavour   2 encircle   3 encounter   4 endure

> When you add a prefix, just add it!
> Don't worry if this doubles some of the letters.
> For example: **un + necessary = unnecessary**
> Don't be tempted to leave out one of the **n**'s.

Copy into your book all the words that have double letters as a result of adding these prefixes.

| | | | | |
|---|---|---|---|---|
| 1 un | + | necessary | intentional | named |
| | | natural | nerve | tidy |
| 2 im | + | possible | mature | modest |
| | | movable | measurable | mobile |
| 3 dis | + | satisfy | similar | obey |
| | | service | trust | appear |
| 4 over | + | rule | look | ripe |
| | | run | reach | react |

35

# Check-up 2

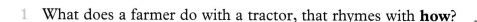

**A** Write a one-word answer for each question.

1 What does a farmer do with a tractor, that rhymes with **how**?

2 What is one less than one, and rhymes with **sort**?

3 What is on the end of your neck, and rhymes with **red**?

4 What do all birds have, that rhymes with **weather**?

5 What surrounds a garden, and rhymes with **sense**?

6 What do we use to cross a river, that rhymes with **fridge**?

**B** Write three words that have a soft **c** and three that have a hard **c**.

**C** Finish these words using *er*, *or* or *ar*.

1 comput_____  2 popul_____  3 calculat____  4 build_____

5 circul _____  6 instruct____  7 strang_____  8 simil_____

**D** Add *un* or *in* to finish these words.

1 ___tidy  2 ___correct  3 ___done  4 ___complete

36

A  Finish these words by adding *ance, ence* or *ince*.

1 f_____    2 s_____    3 ch_____    4 pr_____

5 sent_____    6 off_____    7 entr_____    8 m_____

B  Add *ing* to each of these words.
You will need to make other changes as well.

1 judge    2 bridge    3 cadge    4 hedge    5 dodge

C  Finish these words by adding *ary, ery* or *ory*.

1 secret_____    2 necess_____    3 fact_____    4 discov_____

5 myst_____    6 vict_____    7 machin_____    8 ordin_____

D  Write the **antonym** (opposite) for each of these by choosing the prefix **un, in** or **im**.

1 accurate    2 kind    3 perfect    4 happy    5 complete

A  Write a word to rhyme with each of these.
Each of your answer words must contain the **ough** letter pattern.
1 bluff    2 toff    3 toe    4 cow

B  Make a word web using the word **head**.
Find as many words in the same family as you can.

C  Write the root word for each of these.
1 bouncing    2 announcing    3 prancing
4 convincing    5 commencing

D  Complete these words using *dge* or *ge*.

1 hu_____    2 bri_____    3 ju_____    4 slu_____    5 colle_____

E  Arrange the words in each of these groups in alphabetical order.
1 regulation  regulate  irregular  regulating
2 radiate  radiation  radiator  radiating

37

# ous
# ious

SPELLING *Focus*

victor**ious**

## key words

| | |
|---|---|
| **look** | dangerous |
| | enormous |
| **say** | famous |
| | generous |
| | jealous |
| | nervous |
| **cover** | |
| | curious |
| | furious |
| **write** | previous |
| | serious |
| | various |
| **check** | victorious |

*(column labels down the sides: look, say, cover, write, check)*

Copy these sentences into your book. Fill the gaps with words from the key word list.

1 I really would like to be a f____ racing driver.

2 It might be d____ , but it would be exciting.

3 My family would be n____ as they watched me.

4 They would be proud if I was the v____ driver and won the World Championship!

**A** Match these adjectives with their nouns.
Write them in pairs in your book.

| nouns | adjectives |
|-------|------------|
| danger | suspicious |
| jealousy | victorious |
| victory | nervous |
| nerve | disastrous |
| disaster | jealous |
| suspicion | dangerous |

**B** Add at least another four pairs to your list.

SPELLING *Extension*

When adding the suffix **ous** or **ious** to words ending
with **our**, first drop the **u** in the word to which the
suffix is added, like this:

   **vapour   vaporous**

**A** Add *ous* or *ious* to each of these words, and then use
each one in a sentence that shows its meaning.

1 victor        2 labour        3 vigour        4 glamour

**B** Some **ious** words can be particularly troublesome.
Copy these into your book, and underline the final
letter **i** in each. Any that you think you might forget,
write three times each!

curious        vicious        anxious        conscious        precious

delicious        religious        suspicious        cautious        gracious

Now ask a friend to test you.

# a

## and double letters

**key words**

| look say cover write check |
| --- |
| accurate |
| allow |
| allergy |
| announce |
| anniversary |
| apple |
| appear |
| arrest |
| arrive |
| assistant |
| assembly |
| attack |
| attention |

A **canner** exceedingly **canny**
One morning remarked to his **granny**,
"A **canner** can can
Anything that he can,
But a **canner** can't can a can, can he?"

**A** Match a key word to each of these pictures.
Write the answers in your book.

1 att_____    2 att_____    3 ass_____

4 arr_____    5 app_____    6 arr_____

**B** Write sentences using two of these words.

40

Hidden in the wordsearch are the answers to these riddles.
Write out the answers in your book.

| a | n | n | i | v | e | r | s | a | r | y |
|---|---|---|---|---|---|---|---|---|---|---|
| t | a | c | a | t | t | a | c | k | f | z |
| t | b | a | s | s | i | s | t | a | n | t |
| e | x | p | s | a | d | w | e | f | z | r |
| n | q | p | e | l | m | a | c | e | d | l |
| t | o | e | m | l | a | r | r | e | s | t |
| i | p | a | b | o | q | z | l | t | v | u |
| o | w | r | l | w | d | f | y | q | r | l |
| n | p | z | y | x | e | u | a | b | e | x |

1 Take off **ap** and you have a fruit.
2 Drop **at** and **ion** and you have something for camping.
3 A small nail is the last part of this word.
4 The front of this word (that ends with **y**) looks like a small horse.
5 The end of this word is the opposite of 'high'.
6 If you're tired you'll like the last four letters of this word.
7 The last three letters are a tiny creature.
8 This happens every year.

Remember, a **syllable** is a part of a word that can be said by itself. Each syllable has its own vowel sound, like this:

'annoy' is pronounced **an - noy**, so it has two syllables.

'attention' is pronounced **at - ten - tion**, so it has three syllables.

Copy these words. Sort them into lists of one-syllable, two-syllable and three-syllable words.

1 *appear*   2 *attack*   3 *attempting*   4 *all*   5 *assistant*
6 *assembly*   7 *annual*   8 *arranging*   9 *allow*   10 *applaud*

Does each of your syllables have a vowel sound?

For example:

| 1 syllable | 2 syllables | 3 syllables |
|---|---|---|
| add | adding | addition |

41

# ent
# ence
# ant
# ance

SPELLING *Focus*

**key words**

*look say cover write check*

silent
silence
evident
evidence
violent
violence
different
difference

distant
distance
important
importance
assistant
assistance

*check write cover say look*

Silent eleph**ant**,
Obedi**ent** eleph**ant**,
Intellig**ent** eleph**ant**,
Viol**ent** eleph**ant** …

Dist**ant** eleph**ant**!!

Copy these sentences into your book.
Add the missing endings.

1  There was no noise. It was totally s____.
2  The police said they could find no evid____.
3  This argument won't be settled by viol____.
4  We will be going to a differ____ school next year.
5  The shop assist____ was very helpful.
6  Her discovery was of great import____.

**A** Match these adjectives with their nouns.
Write them in pairs in your book.

| adjectives | nouns |
|---|---|
| distant | silence |
| silent | distance |
| innocent | ignorance |
| obedient | intelligence |
| ignorant | obedience |
| intelligent | innocence |

**B** Make a noun from each of these adjectives. Write them out.

1 fragrant  2 important  3 absent  4 evident

5 convenient  6 violent  7 abundant  8 different

Adverbs describe actions. Many adverbs are made by adding **ly** to a noun, like this:

**efficient + ly = efficiently**

Copy these into your book.

effici_____  sil_____  frequ_____  import_____

viol_____  abund_____  intellig_____  innoc_____

1 Add *ent* or *ant* to each one to make an adjective.
2 Make an adverb from each adjective.
3 Write a phrase or short sentence to use each adverb you have made.

43

# tricky words 1

## *Focus*

SPELLING

### key words

look say cover write check

check write cover say look

write
scissors
wrist
build
thistle

receive
believe
chief
eight

difficult
area
quarrel

address

castle
scenery
guard
guitar
listen
wrist
wreck
wrong    biscuit
6×9=56
write    Dear Rosie
muscle
scent
whistle
thistle
build
scissors

Copy these words into your book. Underline the letters which you think someone might forget to put in.

This rule will help you remember whether the **i** comes **before** or **after** the **e**.

**i** comes **before e** (when the sound is 'ee') –
   p**ie**ce, rel**ie**f

**except** after **c** – rec**ei**ve, c**ei**ling

**or** when the sound is **not** 'ee' – forf**ei**t, r**ei**gn

Copy these words into your book, choosing **ie** or **ei** to fill the gaps.

1 rec__ve    2 th__r    3 sl__ght    4 f__ld    5 dec__t

6 l__sure    7 bel__ve    8 r__n    9 ach__ve    10 w__ld

11 ch__f    12 sh__ld    13 v__n    14 __ght    15 rec__pt

SPELLING *Extension*

**A** Look carefully at these words.
All of the double consonants have been taken out.
Think carefully about which should be 'double letters'. Write them correctly in your book.
Use a dictionary to check your final list.

1 exagerate    2 inocent    3 ocupy    4 ocasion    5 paralel

6 posesions    7 sudenes    8 woolen    9 adres    10 vacinate

**B** A pair of consonants is missing from each gap.
Copy the words, adding the missing letters.

1 a__o__odation    a place to live

2 a__ition    adding up

3 a__re__    name of where you live

4 co__i__ee    organised group of people

5 disa__oint    be below expectations

6 di__icult    not easy

45

# tricky words 2

where's   what's   who's

**key words**

look say cover write check

I'm
we're
can't
isn't

valuable
lovable
recognisable
noticeable

asthma
telescope
geography
paralyse

---

I'm I'll I've I'd we'll we've we're
isn't weren't wasn't
wouldn't won't can't
it's what's where's who's

**A** Match a contraction from the box with these pairs of words. Write them in your book. The first is done to help you.

1 I am = I'm   2 is not =   3 who is =

4 what is =   5 I would =   6 we are =

7 will not =   8 where is =   9 we will =

10 it is =   11 I will =

**B** What are these contractions short for?

1 I'd =   2 I'll =   3 I've =   4 hadn't =

5 we'll =   6 they've =   7 isn't =   8 weren't =

9 wouldn't =   10 won't =   11 can't =   12 what's =

When adding the suffix **able** to a word that ends with **e**, we nearly always first drop the **e**.

Example: **value + able = valuable**

But there are some important exceptions!

Use your dictionary to spot the four words in this group that must keep their final **e** when **able** is added. Write all the answers in your book.

1 value + able =

2 change + able =

3 cure + able =

4 peace + able =

5 believe + able =

6 recognise + able =

7 love + able =

8 notice + able =

9 desire + able =

10 service + able =

All of the words in the list below came into English from the Greek language. They therefore have slightly unusual spelling patterns.

One letter is omitted from each word. Write each word correctly in your book.

1 r_ubarb

2 r_eumatism

3 cata_rh

4 ast_ma

5 paral_se

6 _sychology

7 g_ography

8 g_ometry

9 archa_ology

10 autobiogra_hy

11 micr_scope

12 tel_scope

13 catastroph_

14 apostroph_

15 enc_clopedia

# Check-up 3

Find the missing letters. Write the complete words in your book.

1 fam_us   2 danger_us   3 victor_ous   4 ser_ous

5 ac_urate   6 as_embly   7 differ_nt   8 import_nt

9 rece_ve   10 oc_asion   11 instruc_ion   12 autogra_

## SPELLING *Extra*

A  Write these words in your book, adding either **ie** or **ei** as necessary.

1 rec__pt   2 rec__ve   3 ch__f   4 f__ld   5 __ght

6 bel__ve   7 th__r   8 dec__t   9 sh__ld   10 l__sure

B  Each of these words has an incorrect extra letter. Write them correctly into your book.

1 loveable   2 recogniseable   3 valueable   4 cureable

5 believeable   6 unmistakeable   7 undesireable

## SPELLING *Extension*

A  Copy these words, dividing them into syllables as you do. The first one is done for you.

1 attempted   at-temp-ted   2 arrangement

3 additional   4 appearance   5 arrested

B  Copy these words into your book, adding the missing letter or letters.

1 q_ar_el   2 embar_as_ment   3 _sych_logist

4 g_ogra_hy   5 ast_matic   6 exa_gera_ion

7 para_lel   8 vac_ination   9 a_dress

10 r_ubarb   11 r__umatism   12 apostr_ph_